THIS BELONGS TO

IF LOST, PLEASE RETURN TO:

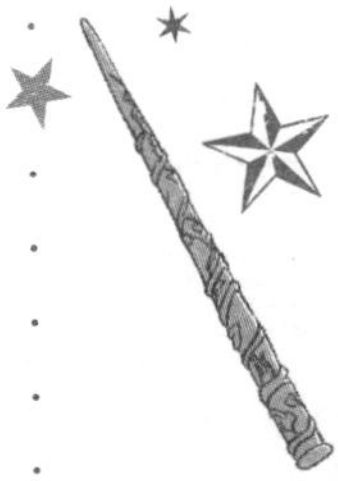

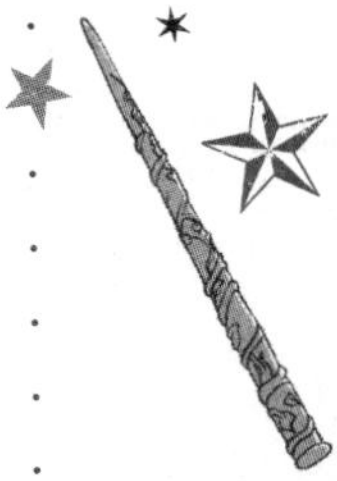

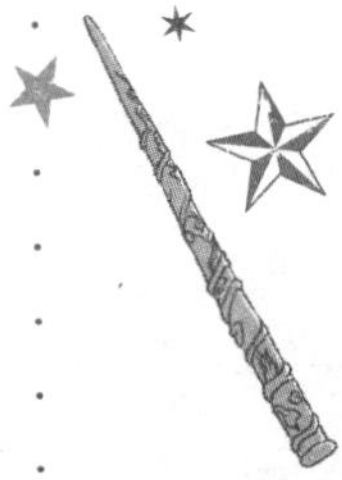

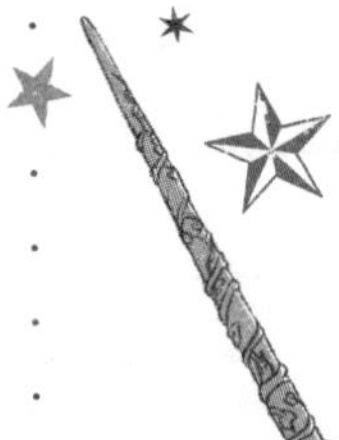

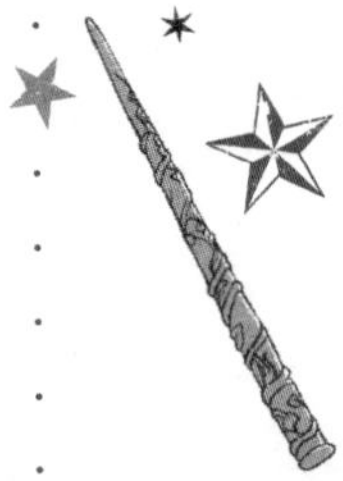

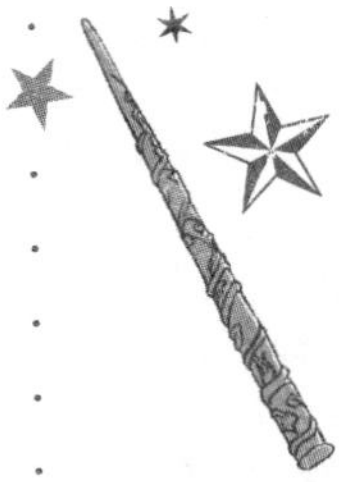

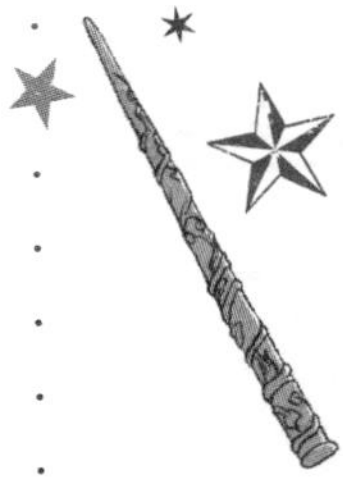

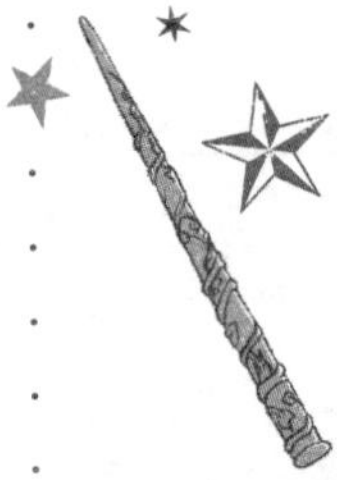

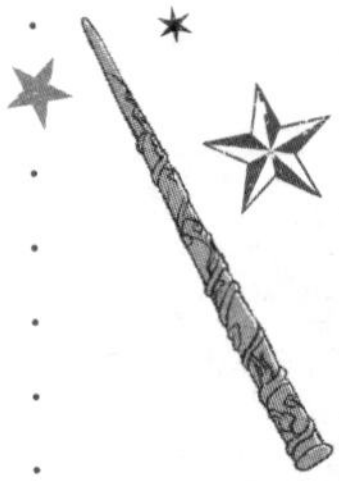

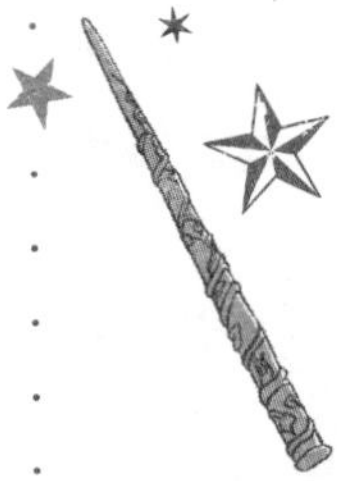

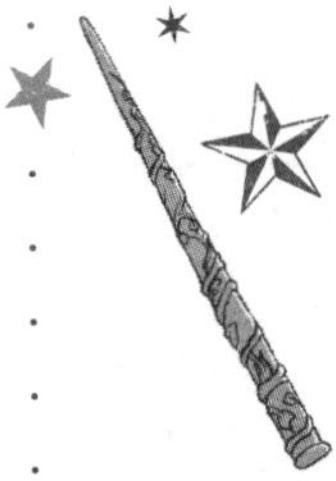

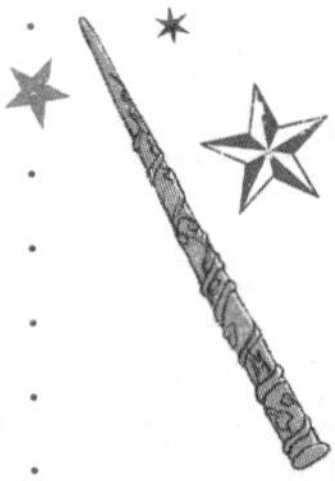

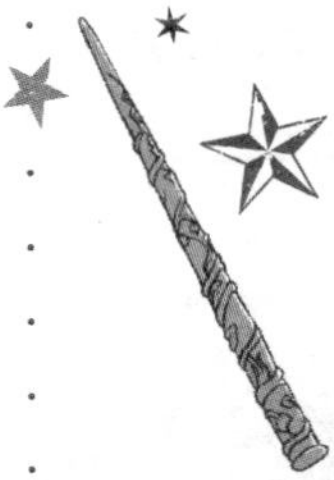

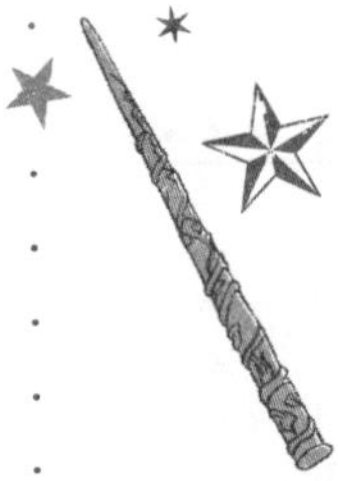

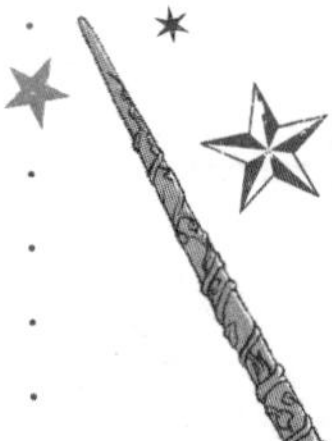

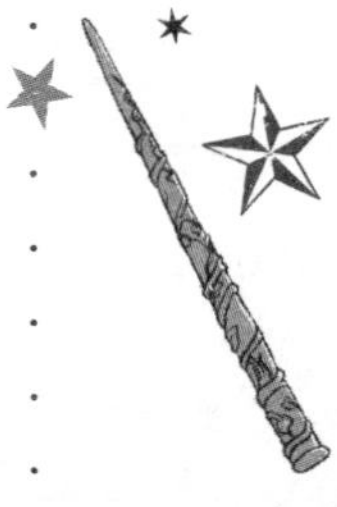

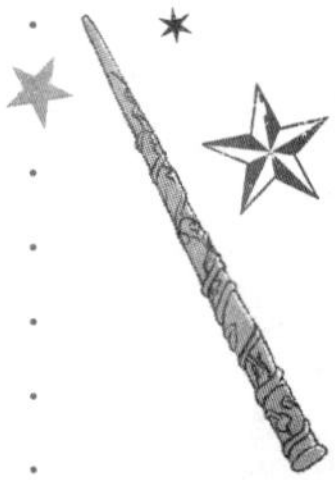

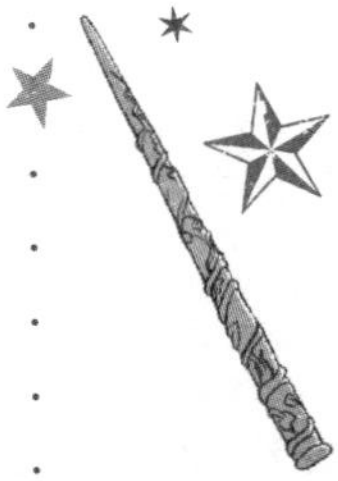

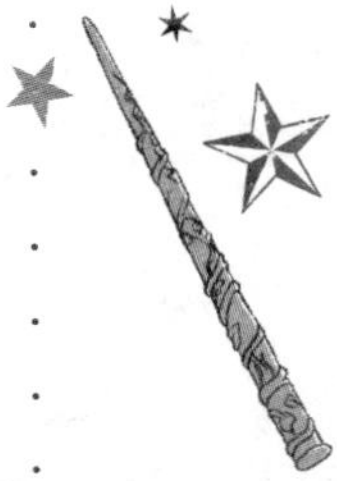

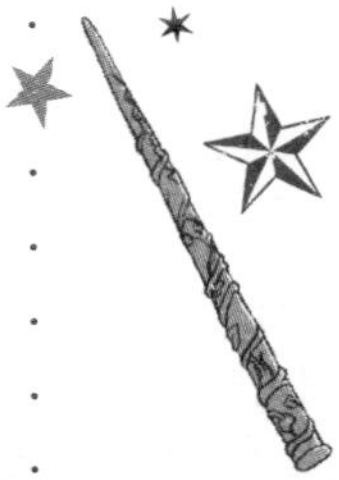

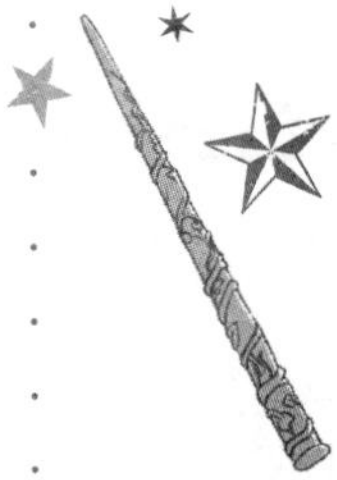

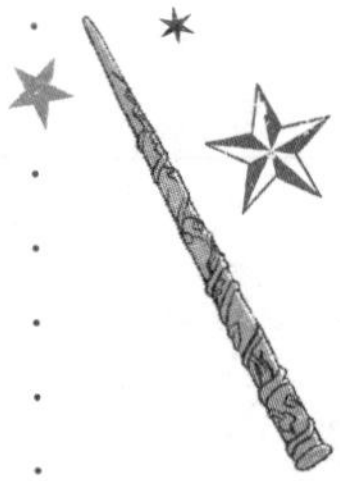

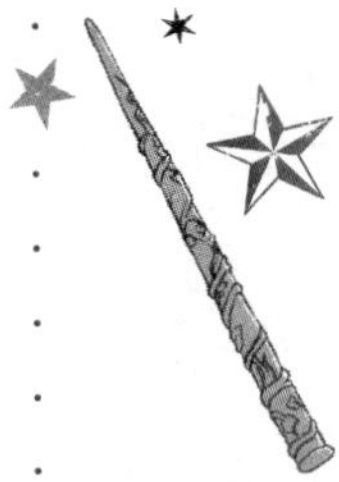

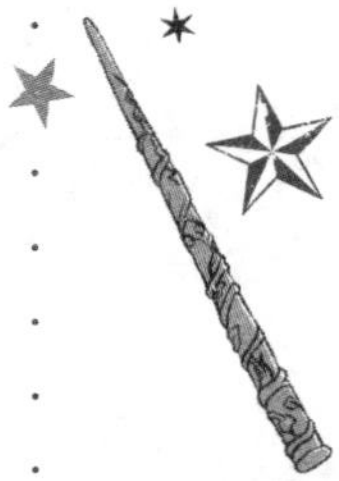

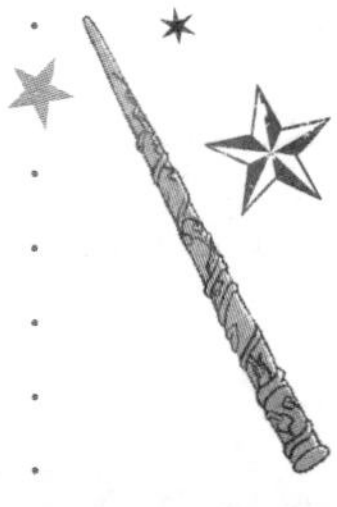

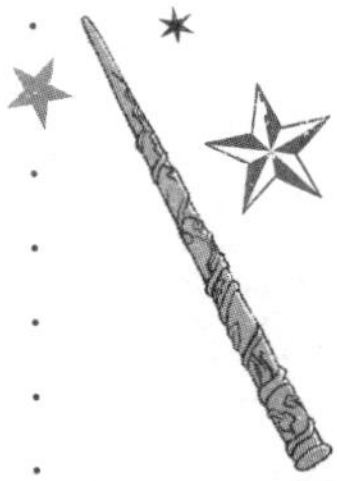

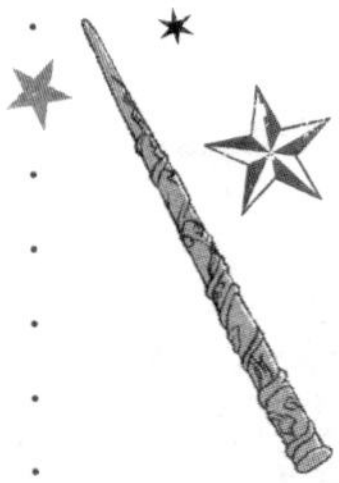

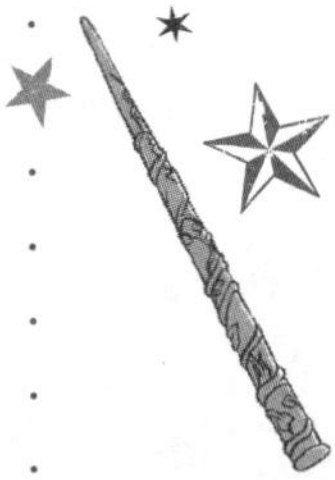

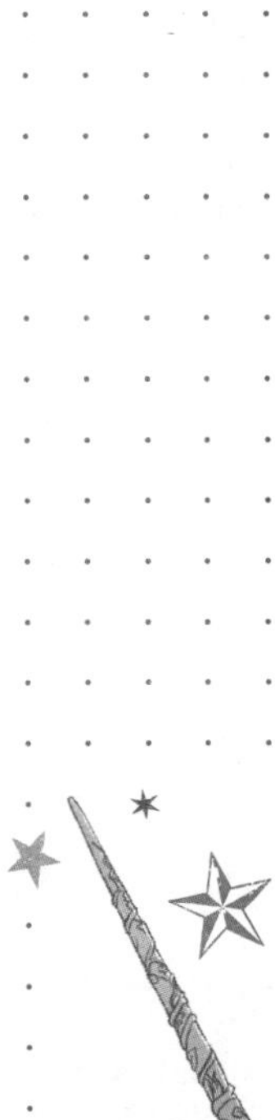

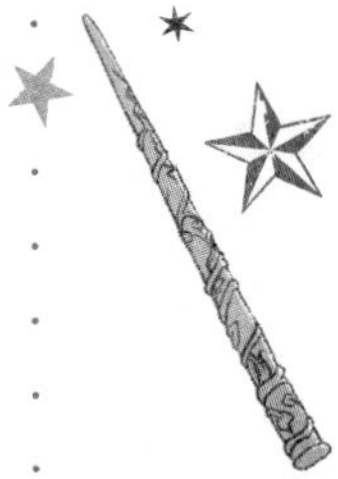

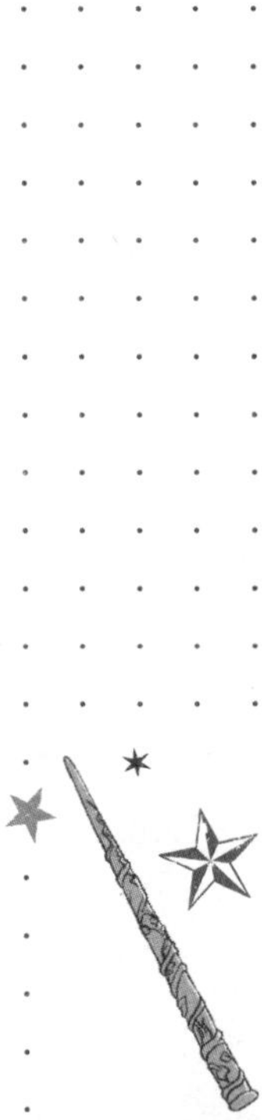

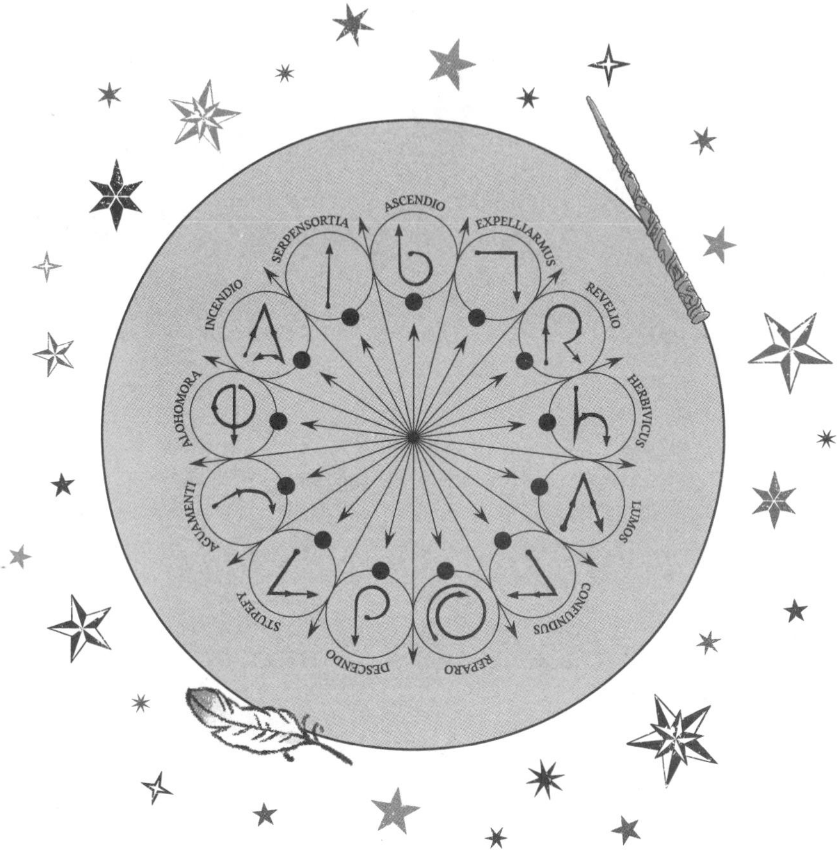

Harry Potter

INSIGHTS

www.insighteditions.com

MANUFACTURED IN CHINA

10 9 8 7 6 5 4 3 2 1